EASY AIR FRYER RECIPES

Over 50 Super Healthy Recipes For Your Everyday Meals

SANDY LEWIS

Legal Notice:

Disclaimer Notice:

Table of Contents

INTRODUCTION

Air fryers work by cooking food with the circulation of hot air. This is what makes the foods you put into it so crispy when they come out! Something called the "Maillard Effect" happens, which is a chemically induced reaction that occurs to the heat that makes it capable for this fryer to brown foods in such a short time, while keeping nutrients and flavor intact.

The Benefits of Using an Air Fryer

A massive reduction in oil –no more than a tsp or two of foil is needed to cook food in an air fryer and yet it still achieves the same texture. A far cry from the many cups of oil that you would have to use to cook food in a deep fryer. The result is food that is not soaked in unhealthy fat that will clog the arteries.

Bursting with flavor – the flavor of the food truly comes out in an air fryer. Despite the small amount of oil used in "frying" the food, the "fried" taste and texture is achieved.

Easy press-and-go operation –No longer do you need to watch over your frying pan on your stove while frying your food. This also means no splattering of oil and accidental burns. All of the magic happens in the cooking chamber, just set your cooking preferences, push the right button, and let the air fryer do all of the work.

Rapid cooking times –The high temperatures that are circulated in the cooking chamber cut common cooking times in half. This is because the heat is maintained throughout the time being cooked meaning you do not have to worry about the loss of heat slowing down your cooking.

Cleaning made Easy –With food baskets that are dishwasher safe, it's as simple as removing it and putting it in. The cooking chamber can easily be cleaned with a cloth and a mild dishwashing soap.

Versatile unmatched – this modern appliance is more than just a fryer. You can bake, grill, and broil in it too. More of a highly versatile, mini convection oven rather than a fryer.

Safe – Its components are food safe and the cooking process itself helps you avoid kitchen accidents that can result in oil burns. The body of the air fryer hardly gets hot even if the temperature inside is at its highest. Using your standard kitchen gloves will give you more than enough protection when handling this kitchen appliance.

These benefits make air fryers the obvious choice when it comes to healthy cooking No compromise on flavor or convenience!

To dumb it down, air fryers can do what those oil fryers do, but in a much healthier way than submerging food into greasy and fattening oil.

Getting the Most Out of your Air Fryer

To maximize the benefits of using an air fryer, here are some tips that you should not overlook:

Getting Started

- Place your air fryer on a level and heatproof kitchen top, if you have granite surfaces this is perfect.
- Avoid putting it close to the wall as this will dissipate the heat causing slower cooking times. Leave a space of at least five inches between the wall and the air fryer.

• Oven-safe baking sheets and cake pans may be used in the air fryer on the condition that they can fit inside easily and the door can close.

Before Cooking

• If you can, always preheat your air fryer for 3 minutes before cooking. Once the timer goes off it will be ready to rock and roll.

• Use a hand pumped spray bottle for applying the oil. Adopting this method will cause you to use less oil and is an easier option when compared to brushing or drizzling. Avoid canned aerosol brands as they tend to have a lot of nasty chemicals

• Always Bread if necessary. This breading step should not be missed. Be sure to press the breading firmly onto the meat or vegetable so the crumbs do not fall off easily.

Whilst Cooking

• Adding water to the air fryer drawer while cooking high-fat foods to will prevent excessive smoke and heat. Use this technique when cooking burgers, bacon, sausage and similar foods.

• Secure light foods such as bread slices with toothpicks so they don't get blown around.

• Avoid putting too many food items into the air fryer basket. Overcrowding will result in uneven cooking and will also prevent the food from getting that glorious crispy texture that we all love.

• Shaking the fryer and flipping the food halfway through the cooking process is advised to make sure that everything inside cooks evenly.

• Opening the air fryer a few times to check how the food is doing won't affect the cooking time, so don't worry.

Once done:

• Remove the basket from the drawer before taking out the food to prevent the oil remaining on the food that you just fried.

• The juices in the air fryer drawer can be used to make delicious marinades and sauces. If you find it too greasy you can always reduce it in a saucepan to get rid of the excess liquid.

• Cleaning both the basket and drawer after every use is imperative.

Now that you've gotten to know the basics of using the air fryer, let's get to the exciting part—it's cooking time!

BREAKFAST

1. Fluffy Cheesy Omelet

Preparation Time: 10 minutes

Cooking time: 15 minutes

Servings: 2

INGREDIENTS:

- 4 eggs
- 1 large onion, sliced
- 1/8 cup cheddar cheese, grated
- 1/8 cup mozzarella cheese, grated
- Cooking spray
- ¼ teaspoon soy sauce
- Freshly ground black pepper, to taste

DIRECTIONS:

1. Preheat the Air fryer to 360 o F and grease a pan with cooking spray.
2. Whisk together eggs, soy sauce and black pepper in a bowl.
3. Place onions in the pan and cook for about 10 minutes.
4. Pour the egg mixture over onion slices and top evenly with cheese.
5. Cook for about 5 more minutes and serve.

NUTRITION: Calories: 216; Fat: 13.8g; Carbs: 7.9g; Sugar: 3.9g; Protein: 15.5g;

2. Crust-Less Quiche

Preparation Time: 5 minutes

Cooking time: 30 minutes

Servings: 2

INGREDIENTS:

- 4 eggs
- ¼ cup onion, chopped
- ½ cup tomatoes, chopped
- ½ cup milk
- 1 cup Gouda cheese, shredded
- Salt, to taste

DIRECTIONS:

1. Preheat the Air fryer to 340 o F and grease 2 ramekins lightly.
2. Mix together all the ingredients in a ramekin until well combined.
3. Place in the Air fryer and cook for about 30 minutes.
4. Dish out and serve.

NUTRITION: Calories: 348; Fat: 23.8g; Carbs: 7.9g; Sugar: 6.3g; Protein: 26.1g;

3. Stuffed Portobello Mushrooms with Ground Beef

Preparation Time: 10 minutes

Cooking time: 13 minutes

Servings: 3

INGREDIENTS:

- 3 Portobello mushrooms
- ½ cup ground beef
- 1 teaspoon minced garlic
- 1 oz onion, chopped
- 1 teaspoon olive oil
- ¾ teaspoon ground nutmeg
- ¾ teaspoon cilantro

DIRECTIONS:

1. Put the ground beef in the mixing bowl.
2. Add minced garlic and chopped onion.
3. After this, add ground nutmeg and cilantro.
4. Mix the mixture up carefully.
5. Fill the mushrooms with the ground beef mixture.
6. Then sprinkle the mushrooms with the olive oil and wrap them in the foil.
7. Put the wrapped mushrooms in the air fryer basket and cook for 10 minutes at 380 F.
8. Then discard the foil from the mushrooms and cook them for 3 minutes more at 400 F.
9. Chill the cooked meal little and serve!

NUTRITION: Calories: 42; Fat: 1.8g; Fiber: 1.3g; Carbs: 4.5g; Protein: 3.3g;

4. Fish Fritatta

Preparation Time: 10 minutes

Cooking time: 15 minutes

Servings: 3

INGREDIENTS:

- 1 tablespoon fresh dill, chopped
- 1 tablespoon fresh parsley, chopped
- ¼ teaspoon ground nutmeg
- 2 tablespoons coconut milk
- 4 eggs
- 8 oz fillet chopped

DIRECTIONS:

1. Beat the eggs in the mixing bowl and whisk well.
2. Add chopped salmon and fresh dill.
3. Add fresh parsley and ground nutmeg.
4. Stir the mixture gently and add coconut milk.
5. After this, pour the frittata mixture in the air fryer basket and cook for 15 minutes at 360 F.
6. When the meal is cooked – chill it little and serve!

NUTRITION: Calories: 211; Fat: 13g; Fiber: 0.4g; Carbs: 17g; Protein: 22.5g;

5. Egg Whites with Sliced Tomatoes

Preparation Time: 10 minutes

Cooking time: 15 minutes

Servings: 2

INGREDIENTS:

- 1 tomato, sliced
- 2 egg whites
- ¼ teaspoon ground paprika
- ¼ teaspoon salt
- 1 teaspoon olive oil
- 1 teaspoon dried dill

DIRECTIONS:

1. Pour the olive oil in the air fryer.
2. Then add the egg whites.
3. Sprinkle the egg whites with the salt, dried dill, and ground paprika.
4. Cook the egg whites for 15 minutes at 350 F.
5. When the egg whites are cooked – let them chill little.
6. Place the layer of the sliced tomatoes on the plate.
7. Then chop the egg whites roughly and place over the tomatoes.
8. Serve!

NUTRITION: Calories: 45; Fat: 2.5g; Fiber: 0.5g; Carbs: 1,9g; Protein: 4g;

6. Mustard Chicken Thighs

Cooking time: 35 minutes

Servings: 4

INGREDIENTS:

- 1 ½ lb. chicken thighs, bone-in
- tbsp. Dijon mustard
- Cooking spray
- A pinch of salt and black pepper

DIRECTIONS:

1. Take a bowl and mix the chicken thighs with all the other ingredients and toss.
2. Put the chicken in your Air Fryer's basket and cook at 370°F for 30 minutes shaking halfway. Serve

NUTRITION: Calories: 253; Fat: 17g; Fiber: 3g; Carbs:6g; Protein: 12g;

7. Tomato and Avocado

Preparation Time: 8 minutes

Servings: 4

INGREDIENTS:

- ½ lb. cherry tomatoes; halved
- avocados, pitted; peeled and cubed
- 1 ¼ cup lettuce; torn
- 1/3 cup coconut cream
- A pinch of salt and black pepper
- Cooking spray

DIRECTIONS:

1. Grease the air fryer with cooking spray, combine the tomatoes with avocados, salt, pepper and the cream and cook at 350°F for 5 minutes shaking once
2. In a salad bowl, mix the lettuce with the tomatoes and avocado mix, toss and serve.

NUTRITION: Calories: 226; Fat: 12g; Fiber: 2g; Carbs: 4g; Protein: 8g;

8. Lemony Endive Mix

Preparation time: 10 minutes

Cooking time: 10 minutes

Servings: 4

INGREDIENTS:

- 8 endives, trimmed
- Salt and black pepper to the taste
- tablespoons olive oil
- Juice of ½ lemon
- 1 tablespoon tomato paste
- tablespoons parsley, chopped
- 1 teaspoon stevia

DIRECTIONS:

1. In a bowl, combine endives with salt, pepper, oil, lemon juice, tomato paste, parsley and stevia, toss, place endives in your air fryer's basket and cook at 365 degrees F for 10 minutes.
2. Divide between plates and serve.

NUTRITION: Calories: 160; Fat: 4g; Fiber: 7g; Carbs: 9g; Protein: 4g;

9. Simple Italian Veggie Salad

Preparation time: 10 minutes

Cooking time: 10 minutes

Servings: 8

INGREDIENTS:

- 1 and ½ cups tomatoes, chopped
- 3 cups eggplant, chopped
- 2 teaspoons capers
- Cooking spray
- 3 garlic cloves, minced
- 2 teaspoons balsamic vinegar
- 1 tablespoon basil, chopped
- A pinch of salt and black pepper

DIRECTIONS:

1. Grease a pan that fits your air fryer with cooking spray, add tomatoes, eggplant, capers, garlic, salt and pepper, place in your air fryer and cook at 365 degrees F for 10 minutes.
2. Divide between plates, drizzle balsamic vinegar all over, sprinkle basil and serve cold.
3. Enjoy!

NUTRITION: Calories: 171; Fat: 3g; Fiber: 1g; Carbs: 8g; Protein: 12g;

SIDES

10. Mashed Cauliflower

Preparation time: 5 minutes

Cooking time: 10 minutes

Servings: 4

INGREDIENTS:

- 1 cauliflower, florets separated and steamed
- Salt and black pepper to taste
- ½ cup veggie stock, heated up
- ½ teaspoon turmeric powder
- 1 tablespoon butter
- spring onions, chopped

DIRECTIONS:

1. In a pan that fits your air fryer, mix the cauliflower with the stock, salt, pepper, and turmeric; then stir well.
2. Place the pan in the fryer and cook at 360 degrees F for 10 minutes.

3. Mash the cauliflower mixture using a potato masher, adding the butter and the spring onions.
4. Stir, divide between plates, and serve.

NUTRITION: Calories: 140; Fat: 2g; Fiber: 6g; Carbs: 15g; Protein: 4g;

11. Parsnips Mash

Preparation time: 10 minutes

Cooking time: 15 minutes

Servings: 4

INGREDIENTS:

- 4 parsnips, peeled and chopped
- Salt and black pepper to taste
- 1 yellow onion, chopped
- ¼ cup sour cream
- ½ cup chicken stock, heated up

DIRECTIONS:

1. In a pan that fits your air fryer, place all ingredients except the sour cream; stir well.
2. Place the pan in the air fryer and cook at 370 degrees F for 15 minutes.
3. Mash the parsnip mixture, adding the sour cream; stir well again.
4. Divide between plates and serve as a side dish.

NUTRITION: Calories: 151; Fat: 3g; Fiber: 6g; Carbs: 11g; Protein: 4g;

12. Carrot Puree

Preparation time: 10 minutes

Cooking time: 15 minutes

Servings: 4

INGREDIENTS:

- 1½ pounds carrots, peeled and chopped
- 1 tablespoon butter, softened
- Salt and black pepper to taste
- 1 cup chicken stock, heated up
- 1 tablespoon honey
- 1 teaspoon brown sugar

DIRECTIONS:

1. In a pan that fits your air fryer, mix the carrots with the stock, salt, pepper, and sugar; stir well.
2. Put the pan into the fryer and cook at 370 degrees F for 15 minutes.
3. Transfer the carrot mixture to a blender, add the butter and the honey, and pulse well.
4. Divide between plates and serve.

NUTRITION: Calories: 100; Fat: 3g; Fiber: 3g; Carbs: 7g; Protein: 6g;

13. Avocado Fries

Cooking Time: 10 minutes

Servings: 4

INGREDIENTS:

- 1-ounce aquafina
- 1avocado, sliced
- ½ teaspoon salt
- ½ cup panko breadcrumbs

DIRECTIONS:

1. Toss the panko breadcrumbs and salt together in a bowl. Pour Aquafina into another bowl.
2. Dredge the avocado slices in Aquafina and then panko breadcrumbs.
3. Arrange the slices in single layer in air fryer basket.
4. Air fry at 390°Fahrenheit for 10-minutes.

NUTRITION: Calories: 263; Fat: 7.4g; Carbs: 6.5g; Protein: 8.2g;

14. Crispy & Crunchy Baby Corn

Cooking Time: 10 minutes

Servings: 4

INGREDIENTS:

- 1 cup almond flour
- 1 teaspoon garlic powder
- ¼ teaspoon chili powder
- 4 baby corns, boiled
- Salt to taste
- ½ teaspoon carom seeds
- Pinch of baking soda

DIRECTIONS:

1. In a bowl, add flour, chili powder, garlic powder, baking soda, carom seed, and salt.
2. Mix well. Pour a little water into the batter to make a nice batter. Dip boiled baby corn into the batter to coat.

3. Preheat your air fryer to 350°Fahrenheit. Line the air fryer basket with foil and place the baby corns on foil.
4. Cook baby corns for 10-minutes.

NUTRITION: Calories: 243; Fat: 9.6g; Carbs: 8.2g; Protein: 10.3g;

15. Tasty Tofu

Cooking Time: 12 minutes

Servings: 4

INGREDIENTS:

- ¼ cup cornmeal
- 15-ounces extra firm tofu, drained, cubed
- Salt and pepper to taste
- 1teaspoon chili flakes
- ¾ cup cornstarch

DIRECTIONS:

1. Line the air fryer basket with aluminum foil and brush with oil. Preheat your air fryer to 370°Fahrenheit.
2. Mix all ingredients in a bowl.
3. Place in air fryer and cook for 12-minutes.

NUTRITION: Calories:246; Fat: 11.2g; Carbs: 8.7g; Protein: 7.6g;

16. Juicy Salmon and Asparagus Parcels

Preparation Time: 5 minutes

Cooking time: 13 minutes

Servings: 2

INGREDIENTS:

- 2 salmon fillets
- 4 asparagus stalks
- ¼ cup champagne
- Salt and black pepper, to taste
- ¼ cup white sauce
- 1 teaspoon olive oil

DIRECTIONS:

1. Preheat the Air fryer to 355 o F and grease an Air fryer basket.
2. Mix all the ingredients in a bowl and divide this mixture evenly over 2 foil papers.
3. Arrange the foil papers in the Air fryer basket and cook for about 13 minutes.
4. Dish out in a platter and serve hot.

NUTRITION: Calories: 32; Fat: 16.6g; Carbs: 4.1g; Sugar: 1.8g; Protein: 36.6g;

17. Amazing Salmon Fillets

Preparation Time: 5 minutes

Cooking time: 7 minutes

Servings: 2

INGREDIENTS:

- 2, 7-ounce>-¾-inch thicksalmon fillets
- 1 tablespoon Italian seasoning
- 1 tablespoon fresh lemon juice

DIRECTIONS:

1. Preheat the Air fryer to 355 o F and grease an Air fryer grill pan.
2. Rub the salmon evenly with Italian seasoning and transfer into the Air fryer grill pan, skin-side up.
3. Cook for about 7 minutes and squeeze lemon juice on it to serve.

NUTRITION: Calories: 88; Fat: 4.1g; Carbs: 0.1g; Sugar: 0g; Protein: 12.9g;

18. Steamed Salmon with Dill Sauce

Preparation Time: 15 minutes

Cooking time: 11 minutes

Servings: 2

INGREDIENTS:

- 1 cup water
- 2, 6-ouncesalmon fillets
- ½ cup Greek yogurt
- 2 tablespoons fresh dill, chopped and divided
- 2 teaspoons olive oil
- Salt, to taste
- ½ cup sour cream

DIRECTIONS:

1. Preheat the Air fryer to 285 o F and grease an Air fryer basket.
2. Place water the bottom of the Air fryer pan.
3. Coat salmon with olive oil and season with a pinch of salt.

4. Arrange the salmon in the Air fryer and cook for about 11 minutes.
5. Meanwhile, mix remaining ingredients in a bowl to make dill sauce.
6. Serve the salmon with dill sauce.

NUTRITION: Calories: 224, Fat: 14.4g; Carbs: 3.6g; Sugar: 1.5g; Protein: 21.2g;

19. Sake Shrimp Mix

Preparation time: 5 minutes

Cooking time: 12 minutes

Servings: 4

INGREDIENTS:

- 1pound shrimp, peeled and deveined
- ½ teaspoon cumin, ground
- 1/3 cup sake
- 1tablespoon soy sauce
- A pinch of cayenne pepper
- 1teaspoon mustard
- 1teaspoon sugar

DIRECTIONS:

1. In a pan that fist your air fryer, mix the shrimp with the sake and the other ingredients, introduce the pan in the fryer and cook at 370 degrees F for 12 minutes.
2. Divide into bowls and serve.

NUTRITION: Calories: 271, Fat: 11g, Fiber: 7g, Carbs: 16g, Protein: 6g

20. Shrimp and Sausage Mix

Preparation time: 5 minutes

Cooking time: 12 minutes

Servings: 4

INGREDIENTS:

- 1 pound shrimp, peeled and deveined
- 1 cup sausages, sliced
- Juice of 1 lime
- 1 tablespoon olive oil
- 1 yellow onion, chopped
- 1 tablespoon chives, chopped

DIRECTIONS:

1. In a pan that fits your air fryer, mix the shrimp with the sausages and the other ingredients, introduce the pan in the air fryer and cook at 380 degrees F for 12 minutes.
2. Divide the mix into bowls and serve.

NUTRITION: Calories: 201; Fat: 6g; Fiber: 7g; Carbs: 17g; Protein: 7g;

21. Clams and Beer Sauce

Preparation time: 10 minutes

Cooking time: 15 minutes

Servings: 4

INGREDIENTS:

- 1 pound clams
- 1 red onion, chopped
- A pinch of salt and black pepper
- ½ teaspoon sweet paprika
- 1 cup beer
- 2 tablespoons cilantro, chopped
- 1 teaspoon olive oil

DIRECTIONS:

1. In a pan that fits your air fryer, mix the clams with the onion and the other ingredients, introduce in the fryer and cook at 390 degrees for 15 minutes.
2. Divide into bowls and serve.

NUTRITION: Calories 231; Fat: 6g; Fiber: 8g; Carbs: 16g; Protein 16g;

POULTRY

---

22. Stuffed Chicken Breast Recipe

Preparation Time: 45 Minutes

Servings: 8

INGREDIENTS:

- Wolfberries-10
- Sesame oil-3 tsp.
- whole chicken -1
- chopped red chilies; -2
- cubed yam-1
- ginger slices-4
- soy sauce-1 tsp.
- Salt and white pepper to the taste

DIRECTIONS:

1. Spice the chicken with salt, pepper, and rub with soy sauce and sesame oil and stuff with wolf berries, yam blocks, chilies, and ginger.
2. Preheat your air fryer to a temperature of 400 °F
3. Introduce your prepared chicken into your air fryer and cook for 20 minutes
4. Again set your air fryer to another temperature of 360 °F and cook prepared chicken for 15 minutes.
5. Carve your chicken is into your ideal shape and after that point, share among plates and serve.

NUTRITION: Calories: 320; Fat: 12g; Protein: 12g; Fiber: 17g; Carbs: 22g;

23. Chicken and Asparagus Stir Fry Recipe

Preparation Time: 30 Minutes

Servings: 4

INGREDIENTS:

- asparagus spears-8
- Ground cumin-1 tsp.
- halved chicken wings-8
- Chopped rosemary -1 tbsp.
- Salt and black pepper to the taste

DIRECTIONS:

1. Firstly, pat dry chicken wings at that point season with salt, cumin, pepper, and rosemary
2. Introduce your prepared chicken into your air fryer's crate and cook at 360 °F, for 20 minutes.
3. On the other hand, preheat a container to over medium warmth, incorporate asparagus at that point include water, spread the dish and permit to steam for a couple of minutes;

4. Transfer the blend to a bowl loaded up with ice water, channel and spot on plates.
5. Serve your chicken wings along with your asparagus.

NUTRITION: Calories: 270; Fat: 8;g Fiber: 12g; Protein: 22g; Carbs: 24g;

24. Lemongrass Turkey

Preparation time: 10 minutes

Cooking time: 20 minutes

Servings: 4

INGREDIENTS:

- ½ cup lemongrass, trimmed and chopped
- 2 pounds turkey breast, skinless, boneless and roughly cubed
- 1 tablespoon balsamic vinegar
- 1 cup coconut cream
- Salt and black pepper to the taste
- 1 tablespoon chives, chopped
- 1 tablespoon lemon juice

DIRECTIONS:

1. In the air fryer's pan, mix the turkey with the lemongrass and the other ingredients, toss, introduce the pan in the fryer and cook at 380 degrees F for 25 minutes.
2. Divide everything between plates and serve.

NUTRITION: Calories: 251; Fat: 8g; Fiber: 14g; Carbs: 19g; Protein: 6g

25. Chicken and Coriander Sauce

Preparation time: 10 minutes

Cooking time: 25 minutes

Servings: 4

INGREDIENTS:

- 2 pounds chicken breast, skinless, boneless and sliced
- 1 cup cilantro, chopped
- Juice of 1 lime
- ½ cup heavy cream
- 1 tablespoon olive oil
- ½ teaspoon cumin, ground
- 1 teaspoon sweet paprika
- 5 garlic cloves, chopped
- 1 cup chicken stock
- A pinch of salt and black pepper

DIRECTIONS:

1. In a blender, mix the cilantro with the lime juice and the other ingredients except the chicken and the stock and pulse well.
2. Put the chicken, stock and sauce in the air fryer's pan, toss, introduce the pan in the fryer and cook at 380 degrees F for 25 minutes.
3. Divide the mix between plates and serve

NUTRITION: Calories: 261; Fat: 12g; Fiber: 7g; Carbs 15g; Protein 25g

MEAT

26. Roasted Lamb Chops

Preparation Time: 29 minutes

Servings: 6

INGREDIENTS:

- 12 lamb chops
- 1 green chili pepper; chopped
- 1 garlic clove; minced
- ½ cup cilantro; chopped
- 3 tbsp. olive oil
- Juice of 1 lime
- A pinch of salt and black pepper

DIRECTIONS:

1. Take a bowl and mix the lamb chops with the rest of the ingredients and rub well.
2. Put the chops in your air fryer's basket and cook at 400°F for 12 minutes on each side.
3. Divide between plates and serve

NUTRITION: Calories: 284; Fat: 10g; Fiber: 3g; Carbs: 6g; Protein: 16;

27. Beef Meatloaf

Preparation Time: 30 minutes

Servings: 4

INGREDIENTS:

- 1 lb. beef meat, ground
- 1 egg, whisked
- 1 yellow onion; chopped
- 1 tbsp. oregano; chopped
- 3 tbsp. almond meal
- 1 tbsp. parsley; chopped
- Cooking spray
- Salt and black pepper to taste.

DIRECTIONS:

1. Take a bowl and mix all the ingredients except the cooking spray, stir well and put in a loaf pan that fits the air fryer
2. Put the pan in the fryer and cook at 390°F for 25 minutes. Slice and serve hot.

NUTRITION: Calories: 284; Fat: 14g; Fiber: 3g; Carbs: 6g; Protein: 18;

28. Crispy Brats

Preparation Time: 20 minutes

Servings: 4

INGREDIENTS:

- 4, 3-oz.beef bratwursts

DIRECTIONS:

1. Place brats into the air fryer basket.
2. Adjust the temperature to 375 Degrees F and set the timer for 15 minutes.

NUTRITION: Calories: 286; Protein: 11.8g; Fiber: 0.0g; Fat: 24.8g; Carbs: 0.0g

29. Nutmeg Lamb

Preparation time: 5 minutes

Cooking time: 30 minutes

Servings: 4

INGREDIENTS:

- 1 pound lamb stew meat, cubed
- 2 teaspoons nutmeg, ground
- 1 teaspoon coriander, ground
- 1 cup heavy cream
- 2 tablespoons olive oil
- 2 tablespoons chives, chopped
- Salt and black pepper to the taste

DIRECTIONS:

1. In the air fryer's pan, mix the lamb with the nutmeg and the other ingredients, put the pan in the air fryer and cook at 380 degrees F for 30 minutes.
2. Divide everything into bowls and serve.

NUTRITION: Calories: 287, Fat: 13g, Fiber: 2g, Carbs: 6g, Protein: 12g

30. Lamb and Eggplant Meatloaf

Preparation time: 5 minutes

Cooking time: 35 minutes

Servings: 4

INGREDIENTS:

- 2 pounds lamb stew meat, ground
- 2 eggplants, chopped
- 1 yellow onion, chopped
- A pinch of salt and black pepper
- ½ teaspoon coriander, ground
- Cooking spray
- 2 tablespoons cilantro, chopped
- 1 egg
- 2 tablespoons tomato paste

DIRECTIONS:

1. In a bowl, mix the lamb with the eggplants of the ingredients except the cooking spray and stir.
2. Grease a loaf pan that fits the air fryer with the cooking spray, add the mix and shape the meatloaf.
3. Put the pan in the air fryer and cook at 380 degrees F for 35 minutes.
4. Slice and serve with a side salad.

NUTRITION: Calories: 263, Fat: 12g, Fiber: 3g, Carbs: 6g, Protein: 15g

31. Beef and Broccoli Mix

Preparation time: 10 minutes

Cooking time: 30 minutes

Servings: 4

INGREDIENTS:

- 1 pound beef stew meat, cubed
- 2 cups broccoli florets
- ½ cup tomato sauce
- 1 teaspoon sweet paprika
- 2 teaspoons olive oil
- 1 tablespoon cilantro, chopped

DIRECTIONS:

1. In your air fryer, mix the beef with the broccoli and the other ingredients, toss, cook at 390 degrees F for 30 minutes, divide into bowls and serve.

NUTRITION: Calories: 281, Fat: 12g, Fiber: 7g, Carbs: 19g, Protein: 20g

32. Scrambled Egg Muffins with Cheese

Preparation Time: 20 minutes

Servings: 6

INGREDIENTS:

- ounces smoked turkey sausage, chopped
- eggs, lightly beaten
- 2 tablespoons shallots, finely chopped
- 2 garlic cloves, minced
- Sea salt and ground black pepper, to taste
- 1 teaspoon cayenne pepper
- 6 ounces Monterey Jack cheese, shredded

DIRECTIONS:

1. Simply combine the sausage, eggs, shallots, garlic, salt, black pepper, and cayenne pepper in a mixing dish.
2. Mix to combine well.
3. Spoon the mixture into 6 standard-size muffin cups with paper liners.
4. Bake in the preheated Air Fryer at 340 degrees F for 8 minutes.
5. Top with the cheese and bake an additional 8 minutes.
6. Enjoy!

NUTRITION: Calories: 234; Fat: 15.7g; Carbs: 5.3g; Protein: 17.6g; Sugars: 0.9g; Fiber: 0.4g

33. Frittata with Porcini Mushrooms

Preparation Time: 40 minutes

Servings: 4

INGREDIENTS:

- 3 cups Porcini mushrooms, thinly sliced
- 1 tablespoon melted butter
- 1 shallot, peeled and slice into thin rounds
- 1 garlic cloves, peeled and finely minced
- 1 lemon grass, cut into 1-inch pieces
- 1/3 teaspoon table salt
- 8 eggs
- 1/2 teaspoon ground black pepper, preferably freshly ground
- 1 teaspoon cumin powder
- 1/3 teaspoon dried or fresh dill weed
- 1/2 cup goat cheese, crumbled

DIRECTIONS:

1. Melt the butter in a nonstick skillet that is placed over medium heat. Sauté the shallot, garlic, thinly sliced

Porcini mushrooms, and lemon grass over a moderate heat until they have softened.

2. Now, reserve the sautéed mixture.
3. Preheat your Air Fryer to 335 degrees F. Then, in a mixing bowl, beat the eggs until frothy.
4. Now, add the seasonings and mix to combine well.
5. Coat the sides and bottom of a baking dish with a thin layer of vegetable spray.
6. Pour the egg/seasoning mixture into the baking dish; throw in the onion/mushroom sauté.
7. Top with the crumbled goat cheese.
8. Place the baking dish in the Air Fryer cooking basket.
9. Cook for about 32 minutes or until your frittata is set.
10. Enjoy!

NUTRITION: Calories: 242; Fat: 16g; Carbs: 5.2g; Protein: 17.2g; Sugars: 2.8g; Fiber: 1.3g

34. Spinach Sauté

Preparation time: 5 minutes

Cooking time: 8 minutes

Servings: 4

INGREDIENTS:

- 2 pounds baby spinach
- 1 tablespoon avocado oil
- 1 cup cherry tomatoes, halved
- 4 scallions, chopped
- Salt and black pepper to the taste
- 1 tablespoon chives, chopped

DIRECTIONS:

1. Heat up the air fryer with the oil at 350 degrees F, add the spinach, tomatoes and the other ingredients, toss and cook for 8 minutes.
2. Divide between plates and serve.

NUTRITION: calories: 190, fat: 4g, fiber: 2g, carbs: 13g, protein: 9g

35. Oregano Asparagus

Preparation time: 5 minutes

Cooking time: 8 minutes

Servings: 4

INGREDIENTS:

- 1 pound asparagus, trimmed
- 2 tablespoons avocado oil
- Salt and black pepper to the taste
- 2 teaspoons balsamic vinegar
- 1 tablespoon oregano, chopped

DIRECTIONS:

1. Heat up the air fryer at 350 degrees F, and mix the asparagus with the oil and the other ingredients in the basket.
2. Cook for 8 minutes, divide between plates and serve.

NUTRITION: calories: 190, fat: 3g, fiber: 6g, carbs: 8g, protein: 4g

36. Cheesy Artichokes

Preparation time: 10 minutes

Cooking time: 14 minutes

Servings: 4

INGREDIENTS:

- 4 artichokes, trimmed and halved
- 1 cup cheddar cheese, shredded
- 2 tablespoons olive oil
- A pinch of salt and black pepper
- 3 garlic cloves, minced
- 1 teaspoon garlic powder

DIRECTIONS:

1. In your air fryer's basket, combine the artichokes with the oil, cheese and the other ingredients, toss and cook at 400 degrees F for 14 minutes.
2. Divide everything between plates and serve.

NUTRITION: calories: 191, fat: 8g, fiber: 2g, carbs: 12g, protein: 8g

37. Cajun Tomatoes and Peppers

Preparation time: 4 minutes

Cooking time: 20 minutes

Servings: 4

INGREDIENTS:

- 1 tablespoon avocado oil
- ½ pound mixed bell peppers, sliced
- 1 pound cherry tomatoes, halved
- 1 red onion, chopped
- A pinch of salt and black pepper
- 1 teaspoon sweet paprika
- ½ tablespoon Cajun seasoning

DIRECTIONS:

1. In a pan that fits the air fryer, combine the peppers with the tomatoes and the other ingredients, put the pan it in your air fryer and cook at 390 degrees F for 20 minutes.
2. Divide the mix between plates and serve.

NUTRITION: Calories: 151, Fat: 3g, Fiber: 2g, Carbs: 4g, Protein: 5g

38. Olives and Sweet Potatoes

Preparation time: 5 minutes

Cooking time: 25 minutes

Servings: 4

INGREDIENTS:

- 1 pound sweet potatoes, peeled and cut into wedges
- 1 cup kalamata olives, pitted and halved
- 1 tablespoon olive oil
- 2 tablespoons balsamic vinegar
- A bunch of cilantro, chopped
- Salt and black pepper to the taste
- 1 tablespoon basil, chopped

DIRECTIONS:

1. In a pan that fits the air fryer, combine the potatoes with the olives and the other ingredients and toss.
2. Put the pan in the air fryer and cook at 370 degrees F for 25 minutes.
3. Divide between plates and serve.

NUTRITION: Calories: 132, Fat: 4g, Fiber: 2g, Carbs: 4g, Protein: 4g

39. Lemon Tomatoes

Preparation time: 5 minutes

Cooking time: 20 minutes

Servings: 4

INGREDIENTS:

- 2 pounds cherry tomatoes, halved
- 1 teaspoon sweet paprika
- 1 teaspoon coriander, ground
- 2 teaspoons lemon zest, grated
- 2 tablespoons olive oil
- 2 tablespoons lemon juice
- A handful parsley, chopped

DIRECTIONS:

1. In the air fryer's pan, mix the tomatoes with the paprika and the other ingredients, toss and cook at 370 degrees F for 20 minutes.
2. Divide between plates and serve.

NUTRITION: Calories: 151, Fat: 2g, Fiber: 3g, Carbs 5g, Protein: 5g

40. Peppers and Cheese Dip

Preparation Time: 25 minutes

Servings: 6

INGREDIENTS:

- 2 bacon slices, cooked and crumbled
- 4 oz. parmesan; grated
- 4 oz. mozzarella; grated
- 8 oz. cream cheese, soft
- 2 roasted red peppers; chopped.
- A pinch of salt and black pepper

DIRECTIONS:

1. In a pan that fits your air fryer, mix all the ingredients and whisk really well.
2. Introduce the pan in the fryer and cook at 400°F for 20 minutes. Divide into bowls and serve cold

NUTRITION: Calories: 173; Fat: 8g; Fiber: 2g; Carbs: 4g; Protein: 11g

41. Mozzarella and Tomato Salad

Preparation Time: 17 minutes

Servings: 6

INGREDIENTS:

- 1 lb. tomatoes; sliced
- 1 cup mozzarella; shredded
- 1 tbsp. ginger; grated
- 1 tbsp. balsamic vinegar
- 1 tsp. sweet paprika
- 1 tsp. chili powder
- ½ tsp. coriander, ground

DIRECTIONS:

1. In a pan that fits your air fryer, mix all the ingredients except the mozzarella, toss, introduce the pan in the air fryer and cook at 360°F for 12 minutes
2. Divide into bowls and serve cold as an appetizer with the mozzarella sprinkled all over.

NUTRITION: Calories: 185; Fat: 8g; Fiber: 2g; Carbs: 4g; Protein: 8g

42. Garlic Cheese Dip

Preparation Time: 15 minutes

Servings: 10

INGREDIENTS:

- 1 lb. mozzarella; shredded
- garlic cloves; minced
- 3 tbsp. olive oil
- 1 tbsp. thyme; chopped.
- 1 tsp. rosemary; chopped.
- A pinch of salt and black pepper

DIRECTIONS:

1. In a pan that fits your air fryer, mix all the ingredients, whisk really well, introduce in the air fryer and cook at 370°F for 10 minutes.
2. Divide into bowls and serve right away.

NUTRITION: Calories: 184; Fat: 11g; Fiber: 3g; Carbs: 5g; Protein: 7g

43. Asparagus Wraps

Preparation Time: 20 minutes

Servings: 8

INGREDIENTS:

- 16 asparagus spears; trimmed
- 16 bacon strips
- 1 tbsp. lemon juice
- 2 tbsp. olive oil
- 1tsp. oregano; chopped.
- 1 tsp. thyme; chopped.
- A pinch of salt and black pepper

DIRECTIONS:

1. Take a bowl and mix the oil with lemon juice, the herbs, salt and pepper and whisk well.
2. Brush the asparagus spears with this mix and wrap each in a bacon strip
3. Arrange the asparagus wraps in your air fryer's basket and cook at 390°F for 15 minutes.

NUTRITION: Calories: 173; Fat: 4g; Fiber: 2g; Carbs: 3g; Protein: 6g

44. Zucchini Salsa

Preparation Time: 20 minutes

Servings: 6

INGREDIENTS:

- 1 ½ lb. zucchinis, roughly cubed
- 2 tomatoes; cubed
- 2 spring onions; chopped.
- 1 tbsp. balsamic vinegar
- Salt and black pepper to taste.

DIRECTIONS:

1. In a pan that fits your air fryer, mix all the ingredients, toss, introduce the pan in the fryer and cook at 360°F for 15 minutes
2. Divide the salsa into cups and serve cold.

NUTRITION: Calories: 164; Fat: 6g; Fiber: 2g; Carbs: 3g; Protein: 8g

45. Tomato Bites

Preparation Time: 25 minutes

Servings: 6

INGREDIENTS:

- 6 tomatoes; halved
- 2 oz. watercress
- 3 oz. cheddar cheese; grated
- 1 tbsp. olive oil
- 3 tsp. sugar-free apricot jam
- 2 tsp. oregano; dried
- A pinch of salt and black pepper

DIRECTIONS:

1. Spread the jam on each tomato half, sprinkle oregano, salt and pepper and drizzle the oil all over them
2. Introduce them in the fryer's basket, sprinkle the cheese on top and cook at 360°F for 20 minutes
3. Arrange the tomatoes on a platter, top each half with some watercress and serve as an appetizer.

NUTRITION: Calories: 131; Fat: 7g; Fiber: 2g; Carbs: 4g; Protein: 7g

46. Butter Cookies

Preparation Time: 30 minutes

Servings: 12

INGREDIENTS:

- 2 eggs, whisked
- 2 ¾ cup almond flour
- ¼ cup swerve
- ½ cup butter; melted
- 1 tbsp. heavy cream
- 2 tsp. vanilla extract
- Cooking spray

DIRECTIONS:

1. Take a bowl and mix all the ingredients except the cooking spray and stir well.
2. Shape 12 balls out of this mix, put them on a baking sheet that fits the air fryer greased with cooking spray and flatten them
3. Put the baking sheet in the air fryer and cook at 350°F for 20 minutes
4. Serve the cookies cold.

NUTRITION: Calories: 234; Fat: 13g; Fiber: 2g; Carbs: 4g; Protein: 7g

47. Ginger Cookies

Preparation Time: 25 minutes

Servings: 12

INGREDIENTS:

- ¼ cup butter; melted
- 2 cups almond flour
- 1 cup swerve
- 1 egg
- ¼ tsp. nutmeg, ground
- ¼ tsp. cinnamon powder
- 2 tsp. ginger, grated
- 1 tsp. vanilla extract

DIRECTIONS:

1. Take a bowl and mix all the ingredients and whisk well.
2. Spoon small balls out of this mix on a lined baking sheet that fits the air fryer lined with parchment paper and flatten them

3. Put the sheet in the fryer and cook at 360°F for 15 minutes
4. Cool the cookies down and serve.

NUTRITION: Calories: 220; Fat: 13g; Fiber: 2g; Carbs: 4g; Protein: 3g

48. Creamy Chia Seeds Pudding

Preparation Time: 35 minutes

Servings: 6

INGREDIENTS:

- 2 cups coconut cream
- ¼ cup chia seeds
- egg yolks, whisked
- 1 tbsp. ghee; melted
- 2 tbsp. stevia
- 2 tsp. cinnamon powder

DIRECTIONS:

1. Take a bowl and mix all the ingredients, whisk, divide into 6 ramekins, place them all in your air fryer and cook at 340°F for 25 minutes.
2. Cool the puddings down and serve

NUTRITION: Calories: 180; Fat: 4g; Fiber: 2g; Carbs: 5g; Protein: 7g

49. Orange cake

Preparation Time: 42 Minutes

Servings: 12

INGREDIENTS:

- Orange: 1 peeled and cut to quarters
- Vanilla extract: 1 tbsp
- Eggs: 6
- Orange zest: 2 tbsp
- Cream cheese: 4 oz.
- Baking powder: 1 tbsp
- Flour: 9 oz.
- Sugar: 2 oz. and 2 tbsp
- Yogurt: 4 oz.

DIRECTIONS:

1. Pulse the orange in a food processor
2. Pour in the flour, 2 tbsp sugar, baking powder, eggs and vanilla extract. Pulse it again
3. Place it in 2 spring-form pans.
4. Place it in the air fryer then heat it to 330

5. ° F after which let it cook for 16 minutes.
6. In another bowl, mix cream cheese, orange zest, yogurt and the remaining sugar while stirring
7. Sandwich half of the contents of the bowl between the two cake layers from each spring pan.
8. Spread the half that remained on top of the cake.
9. Serve.

NUTRITION: Calories: 200; Fat: 13; Protein: 8; Carbs: 9g; Fiber: 2g

50. Lemon Cookies

Preparation Time: 30 minutes

Servings: 12

INGREDIENTS:

- ¼ cup cashew butter, soft
- 1 egg, whisked
- ¾ cup swerve
- 1 cup coconut cream
- Juice of 1 lemon
- 1 tsp. baking powder
- 1 tsp. lemon peel, grated

DIRECTIONS:

1. In a bowl, combine all the ingredients gradually and stir well.
2. Spoon balls this on a cookie sheet lined with parchment paper and flatten them.
3. Put the cookie sheet in the fryer and cook at 350°F for 20 minutes
4. Servings the cookies cold

NUTRITION: Calories: 121; Fat: 5g; Fiber: 1g; Carbs: 4g; Protein: 2g

CPSIA information can be obtained
at www.ICGtesting.com
Printed in the USA
LVHW020356010221
677957LV00006BA/227

9 781801 594424